I KNOW AMERICA

Our National Symbols

Linda Carlson Johnson

1928

THE MILLBROOK PRESS

Brookfield, Connecticut

Published by The Millbrook Press
2 Old New Milford Road
Brookfield, CT 06804
© 1992 Blackbirch Graphics, Inc.

Created and produced in association with Blackbirch Graphics.
Series Editor: Bruce S. Glassman

Lib. ed.
10   9   8   7   6   5
Paper ed.
10   9   8   7   6   5   4

Library of Congress Cataloging-in-Publication Data
Johnson, Linda Carlson, 1949–
    Our national symbols / Linda Carlson Johnson.
    Includes bibliographical references and index.
    Summary: Tells the stories behind such well-known national symbols as the Liberty Bell, bald eagle, and Uncle Sam.
    ISBN 1-56294-108-9 (lib. bdg.)   ISBN 1-878841-87-4 (pbk.)
    1. Emblems, National—United States—juvenile literature. [1. Emblems.
2. National.] I. Title. II. Series
JC346.Z3J65   1992
929.9'2'0973—dc20
                                                            91-38893
                                                            CIP
                                                            AC

Special thanks to Elm City Antiques and
Appraisal Service, New Haven, Connecticut.

Thanks also to Battlezone Army and Navy,
New Haven, Connecticut.

Acknowledgments and Photo Credits

Cover: Chuck Peterson; p. 5: ©Bill Bacmann/Stock, Boston, Inc; pp. back cover (Uncle Sam), 6, 8, 10, 16, 17, 19 (all), 20, 24 (all): Library of Congress Collection; p. 12: National Parks Department; p. 14: North Wind Picture Archives; p. 18: ©Stephen Dalton/Photo Researchers, Inc.; p. 26: Culver Pictures, Inc.; pp. 28–29: National Archives; p. 32: ©Henryk T. Kaiser/The Picture Cube; pp. 35, 37: Bettman Archive; p. 36: ©Bruce Glassman; pp. 38, 43: AP/Wide World Photos; p. 40: ©Nik Kleinberg/Stock, Boston, Inc.; p. 44: ©Toby Talbot/AP/Wide World Photos.

Photo Research by **Inge King.**

CONTENTS

What is a symbol? A symbol is something that stands for something else. Numbers and letters are symbols. Numbers stand for amounts, and letters stand for sounds. We use letters and numbers to help other people understand us.

But there are other kinds of symbols too. These kinds of symbols stand for ideas. For example, a tiger is often used as a symbol for strength. A sports team might choose the name "Tigers" to say to other teams, "You'd better watch out for us. We're strong, like tigers." The name also helps the Tigers team members feel that they are strong.

All nations have symbols that become special to their people. One symbol that every nation has is a flag. People display their nation's flag to show pride in their country. This kind of pride is called patriotism. When a nation's flag goes by, its people stand and often salute. Those people are being patriotic.

Other symbols can stand for nations too. A nation's symbols usually belong only to that nation.

What are the symbols that belong only to our country, the United States of America? And how did these things become our national symbols? In this book, you will learn the interesting story of the symbols of America and why they are so important to us as a nation.

Pledging allegiance to our flag is one way we use a symbol to honor our country.

5

SYMBOLS OF A STRUGGLE FOR FREEDOM

Some important symbols of America can be traced back more than two hundred years to the time of our country's birth. At that time, there was no United States of America. There were about 2.5 million people living in the eastern part of what is now the United States. These people mostly lived in thirteen colonies that were ruled by England, a nation across the sea. A governor who reported to the British king was in charge of each colony.

This arrangement worked well for a long time. But in 1763, England was low on money. The British Parliament, which is something like the U.S. Congress today, decided to make the colonists pay taxes.

Opposite:
Angry colonists dressed as Indians threw tea into Boston Harbor in 1773 to protest British taxes. This protest became known as the Boston Tea Party.

7

British soldiers, dressed in red, clash with minutemen at the Battle of Lexington in Massachusetts, in 1775. This battle marked the beginning of the Revolutionary War.

The colonists became very angry about these taxes. They said the taxes were not fair because the colonists did not have a chance to vote for or against them. There were no members of Parliament from the colonies. Mobs of people gathered in many American cities to protest the taxes. In many places, people refused to shop in stores that sold British goods.

When Parliament dropped some of the taxes, people cheered. But soon Parliament voted for new taxes on things such as paint, paper, and tea. The colonists became even more angry. In 1773, a British ship carrying tea from India sailed into Boston Harbor. A group of colonists boarded the ship one night and dumped the tea into the water.

The British Parliament was very angry about what the colonists had done. Parliament voted to close the port of Boston. No trading ships could enter or leave the harbor.

Soldiers Called Minutemen

Soon some Massachusetts towns began to raise their own troops. These armies were called militias. The members of these militias were ordinary people. They were farmers and shopkeepers, fishermen and blacksmiths. One-third of the men in the militia were called minutemen because they had to be ready to fight at a minute's notice.

The minutemen had their first real chance to fight against the British in April 1775. The British learned that the colonists had some weapons and supplies stored at Concord, Massachusetts. Seven hundred British soldiers marched to Concord to destroy these weapons and supplies.

During that night a silversmith named Paul Revere rode through the towns from Boston to Concord. He warned the colonists that the British were coming. Hundreds of minutemen turned out to stop the British. The first shots were fired at Lexington, Massachusetts. All day long, the minutemen fired at the British soldiers. The soldiers were easy targets as they marched in rows in their bright red uniforms. The minutemen hid behind hedges and stone walls, firing again and again with their muskets.

A war against British control over the colonies began that day. That war, which is now called the American Revolution, lasted six years. At the end of the war, a free United States of America was born.

The minutemen of Massachusetts were probably the first symbols of the new American nation. They showed bravery, strength, and readiness to fight for their beliefs. Today, statues of minutemen stand in the Massachusetts towns of Lexington and Concord. These statues are reminders of how our nation began.

A Bell That Rang Out Freedom

Another symbol of our nation's struggle for freedom is the Liberty Bell. This bell was not called the Liberty Bell when it was first used. It was designed and made in Great Britain for the fiftieth anniversary of the Pennsylvania colony. The bell was brought to Philadelphia, Pennsylvania, in 1752. It weighed about one ton (two thousand pounds). It measured about twelve feet at its widest part.

The very first time this big bell rang, it cracked. Bellmakers melted the bell down and recast it. They added different metals

The very first time the Liberty Bell was rung, it cracked.

to make the bell stronger. The new bell worked. People didn't much like the way it sounded, but they said it would have to do.

In the early years, Philadelphia's big bell rang on many special days to call the town's people together. Some people complained that the bell rang too often. They wanted to get rid of it. They said the bell bothered people, especially the sick.

But this bell had a special job to do in 1776. On July Fourth of that year, leaders of all the colonies were in Philadelphia. They approved the Declaration of Independence that day. This paper said that the colonies were breaking away from England to become a free nation. Four days after the Declaration of Independence was signed, it was to be read out loud in public for the first time. The bell we now call the Liberty Bell was rung to bring the people of Philadelphia together to hear that they were free.

On that day when the Liberty Bell rang out for freedom, no one thought it was very special. Few people knew that there were words on the bell. These words had been on the bell for more than twenty years. The words were, "Proclaim liberty throughout the land and unto all the inhabitants thereof." They mean, "Announce freedom all over the land and to all its people."

These words come from the Bible. They were not written about the freedom of the American people. But many years later, people saw how important these words were to their new nation.

Today, the Liberty Bell is housed in a special display near Independence Hall in Philadelphia.

The Liberty Bell Cracks Again

In 1777, British soldiers marched on Philadelphia. People feared that the bell might be stolen by the British and used for scrap metal. So they loaded the heavy bell onto a wagon and took it to the basement of a church in nearby Allentown, Pennsylvania. Once during that rough trip, the bell fell off the wagon. Some people say that the fall may have weakened the bell's metal.

In 1778, the bell was brought back to Philadelphia. It rang out when the Revolutionary War ended and when the U.S. Constitution was signed. And it rang to mark the deaths of many famous Americans. It also rang for the fiftieth anniversary of the signing of the Declaration of Independence.

Then, in 1835, the bell cracked again. Some people say the bell cracked on George Washington's birthday when some little boys pulled too hard on the rope. But most people say it cracked while tolling for the funeral of John Marshall, the chief justice of the United States. The story goes that as the crack ran up the side of the bell, the sound of its ring became higher and higher until it finally fell silent.

It was about this time, in the 1840s, that the bell was first called the Liberty Bell. Soon people began to think of the bell, with its large, jagged crack, as a symbol of America's struggle for freedom.

The Liberty Bell soon became famous. It was displayed many times at fairs and in parades around the country. It made cross-country trips by train and floated down great U.S. rivers by boat. Americans from all across the nation traveled for miles to see it. It no longer rang, but it was still proclaiming "liberty throughout the land."

For many years, the Liberty Bell was always returned to its home, Independence Hall in Philadelphia. Today the bell has its own special building in Philadelphia. A small exhibit in the building tells much of the bell's history. Each year, many thousands of people visit the Liberty Bell, one of the most famous symbols of our nation.

THE BELL FALLS SILENT

In 1846, metalworkers tried to repair the cracked Liberty Bell for George Washington's Birthday. But when the clapper struck the bell, the crack became wider. That was the last time the bell rang. The clapper had to be removed.

The Liberty Bell has not been completely silent since 1846. It has been struck on some important occasions. One of those occasions was the first telephone call made from Pennsylvania to California. On February 22, 1915, three weak chimes of the bell traveled across telephone wires from Philadelphia to San Francisco.

During this telephone call, the mayor of San Francisco pleaded for the bell to make a trip to his city. He said that thousands of schoolchildren had signed petitions. They wanted the bell in San Francisco for a big international fair.

The bell made the trip to San Francisco on a train called the Liberty Bell Special. Wherever the train stopped, thousands of people turned out to see it. Eight million people saw the bell once it was in San Francisco.

SYMBOLS OF
A NEW NATION

One symbol of young America was the United States flag. A year after the American Revolution began in 1776, the thirteen colonies had a flag to unite them in their war against the British. This flag looked much like the flag we have today. It had thirteen stripes of red and white, and the upper left corner was blue with white stars. The first flag had only thirteen stars. Like the thirteen stripes, the stars stood for the first thirteen states. Today, the flag still has thirteen stripes. But it has fifty stars to stand for the fifty states of America.

Opposite:
The first Stars and Stripes was adopted by the Continental Congress on June 14, 1777. The thirteen stars stand for the thirteen original colonies of 1777.

A National Emblem

Another famous American symbol was born in the early days of our nation. That symbol is our national

Benjamin Franklin argued that the wild turkey should be America's national emblem.

emblem, the bald eagle. An emblem is a special symbol that is chosen to stand for an important idea, a nation, or a group of people.

America's Founding Fathers, who wrote our Constitution and began our government, argued for six years about what our national emblem should be. Benjamin Franklin, a famous inventor and leader, wanted the wild turkey to be our national emblem. Franklin complained that the eagle had been the symbol of many other nations in the past. He also said that the eagle is a "bird of bad moral character." Franklin compared the eagle to a criminal, because it steals food from other birds. The turkey, Franklin held, was a more respectable bird. Besides, he said, the turkey was a "true, original native of America."

But Congress did not agree with Franklin. Most members of Congress saw the bald eagle as a symbol of high-flying freedom, strength, and courage. They agreed that the eagle had been a symbol in many other times and in many other places. But they also pointed out that the bald eagle is found only in North America. So the bald eagle could truly be called an American bird.

The Bald Eagle in Trouble

In 1782, when the bald eagle was chosen as our national emblem, there were many thousands of these birds in North America. But as the number of people increased, the number of bald eagles decreased. Some people killed eagles for their feathers. Farmers shot eagles that they thought were killing their chickens. And some people hunted eagles for sport.

As people built cities and towns across America, they took away many of the eagles' nesting places. Then, in the twentieth century, an insect killer called DDT nearly wiped out all the bald eagles in the lower forty-eight states.

This bug killer was sprayed on crops. When it rained, the DDT washed into streams and rivers. Many of the fish in the rivers and the small animals that drank the water got DDT in their bodies. When eagles ate these fish and small animals, the DDT got into the eagles' bodies too. Soon there were so few bald eagles left that they almost became extinct. (*Extinct* means the animal does not exist anymore.)

In the last twenty years, the bald eagle has been making a comeback. After the use of DDT was made illegal, more eagle chicks began to hatch. And new laws protected the eagles' nesting areas and made it a crime to kill a bald eagle. Today, in many places, it is more common for people to spot bald eagles.

Even if you have never seen a wild bald eagle, you probably know what one looks like. The bald eagle is everywhere you look. Brass eagles sit on flagpoles. Pictures of eagles are used on stamps and in magazine and TV ads. And the bald eagle is on another important symbol of America, the Great Seal of the United States.

The bald eagle has long been a symbol of freedom and courage for Americans.

FACTS ABOUT BALD EAGLES

• Bald eagles are not bald. But their white head feathers make them look bald from a distance. Bald eagles get these white feathers when they are about five years old. Before that age the feathers are all brown.

• Male bald eagles weigh up to eight pounds and can have up to a seven-foot wingspan. Female bald eagles are much larger. They can weigh up to twelve pounds and can have a twelve-foot wingspan.

• Eagles have great eyesight. From high in the sky, they can spot a fish in a stream or a small animal moving in the grass. Then they can zoom to earth at speeds of up to two hundred miles per hour to catch their prey (animals for food).

• Bald eagles build huge nests. Some eagle nests are the size and weight of a pickup truck. Eagles use the same nests year after year. They build their nests on cliffs or high in the branches of all trees.

The Great Seal

The Great Seal is a round, two-sided piece of cast metal. It is pressed onto very important papers such as American treaties. Treaties are written agreements between two or more countries.

We see the Great Seal every time we look at a dollar bill. The back of every dollar has drawings of both the front and back of the Great Seal.

Look at a dollar bill so you can see what is on the Great Seal. On the front is a bald eagle. The eagle has a shield across its chest. The shield has thirteen stripes to stand for the first thirteen states.

With the talons, or claws, of one foot, the eagle holds some arrows. These arrows stand for the military might of the United States. With the talons of the other foot, the eagle holds the branch of an olive tree. The olive branch stands for peace.

In its beak, the eagle holds a ribbon with the Latin words *e pluribus unum* written on it. These words mean, "from many, one." This saying shows that the thirteen colonies became one nation when they united. Above the eagle's head is what looks like a cloud filled with thirteen stars. The chief designer of the Great Seal, William Barton, said the stars should look like "a glory, breaking through a cloud."

On the back of the seal, the main picture is a pyramid like those found in Egypt. The pyramid has thirteen layers of stone to stand for the first thirteen states. The stone stands for lasting strength. On the bottom layer of stone is the date of the Declaration of Independence, 1776, in Roman numerals. Above the pyramid is a triangle in a burst of light. Inside the triangle is one large eye, which Barton said was the "All-Seeing Eye" of God.

Above the triangle are the Latin words *annuit coeptis*, which mean "He has favored our undertaking." Below the pyramid are the Latin words *Novus ordo seclorum*, which mean "a new order of the ages."

Top:
One of William Barton's early designs for the Great Seal.

Middle:
The front of the Great Seal.

Bottom:
The back of the Great Seal.

CHAPTER

UNCLE SAM
IS BORN

You have probably seen Uncle Sam. He's a tall, skinny cartoon character in a red, white, and blue suit. He wears a top hat, and he has a pointy white beard.

Uncle Sam, who has the same initials as the United States, stands for the U.S. government and the people of our country. Cartoonists often have Uncle Sam doing something in their drawings, to show what the U.S. government is doing. Or they may use Uncle Sam to show how the people of the United States are feeling.

Uncle Sam didn't exist during the first years after the United States was born. The name *Uncle Sam* was used as early as 1813, but first cartoons of Uncle Sam

Opposite:
The most famous image of Uncle Sam appeared in this poster for the U.S. Army during World War I. It was created by James Montgomery Flagg.

21

didn't appear until the 1830s. There were, however, some characters from the early years of United States history that might have helped to create Uncle Sam.

During the 1750s, the British sometimes called the Americans "Yankees." The Americans took this nickname, along with a popular British tune, and made up their own American character. He was called Yankee Doodle. You probably know the song "Yankee Doodle." It begins,

> Yankee Doodle went to town,
> Riding on a pony;
> Stuck a feather in his cap
> And called it macaroni. . . .

Another character from America's early days was Brother Jonathan. No one knows for sure if Brother Jonathan was a real person, a character in a play, or a name someone made up. But some of the British started to use the name Brother Jonathan to describe all Americans. For example, a British person might say, "Brother Jonathan really got into mischief." What the British person really meant was that the *Americans*, not someone named Brother Jonathan, got into mischief.

Some people say that the cartoon character of Uncle Sam has some of both Yankee Doodle and Brother Jonathan in him. But most people believe that the idea for Uncle Sam came from a real person.

A popular story about Uncle Sam comes from about the time of the War of 1812. In this short war,

THE IMAGE OF UNCLE SAM

Uncle Sam has appeared in thousands of cartoons since the 1830s. During hard times, Uncle Sam looks sad. During happy times, Uncle Sam looks much more cheerful. One famous cartoon of Uncle Sam appeared on the cover of a magazine called the *Saturday Evening Post* in 1927. In that year, an American named Charles Lindbergh made the first airplane flight alone across the Atlantic Ocean. A famous American artist named Norman Rockwell drew Uncle Sam wearing a pilot's helmet. Uncle Sam's short beard was pointed into the wind as he proudly led a fleet of airplanes.

Perhaps the most famous drawing of Uncle Sam is a more serious one. This drawing was used on a poster during World War I. Uncle Sam's face looks directly out of the poster. His arm is stretched out, with his finger pointing toward anyone who looks at the poster. The poster carries the words, "I want YOU for the U.S. Army." This poster helped to get many men to sign up to be soldiers.

the Americans were once again fighting against the British. Many Americans helped with the war effort. One of those Americans was a meat-packer named Sam Wilson, who lived in New York. Wilson supplied meat in barrels to U.S. soldiers. He stamped the initials U.S. on each of his barrels.

As the story goes, one day a visitor came to Wilson's factory. He asked a worker what the initials U.S. on the barrels stood for. The worker replied, "Why, Uncle Sam Wilson." People say that after that time, soldiers began to call their meat Uncle Sam's meat. Later they began to call themselves Uncle Sam's army and say that they were working for Uncle Sam.

Many people believe that Sam Wilson is the person who was the model for Uncle Sam. They say that Sam Wilson is a good person to stand for the United States because he was a hardworking man who loved his country.

Sam Wilson probably did not look anything like the Uncle Sam we see today in cartoons. But that does not really matter. As a symbol, Uncle Sam has taken on an identity of his own. Uncle Sam's red, white, and blue costume is something like one worn during the 1830s by a popular clown. The first cartoons of Uncle Sam did not show him wearing a beard or hat. Those things were added by some artists who drew many cartoons of Uncle Sam during the 1860s and 1870s. These characteristics became an accepted part of the image of Uncle Sam. Some people say the beard and the hat were added to give Uncle Sam a more dignified look. Others say these elements make Uncle Sam look more serious. Whatever the reason, Uncle Sam is unmistakable; his look is one of a kind.

Uncle Sam Wilson died in 1854. But his patriotic spirit lives on in cartoons as an old gentleman who stands for the United States.

Today, the image of Uncle Sam is still used to represent America in political cartoons. Many television commercials use actors dressed up as Uncle Sam to sell everything from hot dogs to automobiles. And the famous "I Want YOU" poster drawn by James Montgomery Flagg is still one of the most common American images around.

THE BISON:
SYMBOL OF THE WEST

The 1800s were a time of great growth in the United States. As the East became more crowded, people packed up their wagons and moved westward. The West was the home of many groups of Native Americans, who had lived in North America for centuries. It was also the home of the American bison, which soon became a symbol of the West for many Americans. Sadly, the bison also became a symbol of a way of life that was destroyed by the white pioneers who settled in the rugged West.

During the 1800s, bison roamed in huge herds all over North America. In 1855, there were from 75 million to 90 million bison. But by 1875, there were

Opposite:
In 1855, the wild American West was filled with huge herds of bison. By some counts, their population was more than 75 million.

27

The bison were an important part of Native American daily life. When Native Americans hunted bison, they only killed as many animals as they could use at one time.

fewer than one thousand bison left. In just twenty years, a huge population of bison had been almost completely wiped out.

The first people traveling west were amazed at how many bison roamed the country. One American army officer described standing on high ground in central Kansas. He said that the land as far as he could see was covered with the huge shaggy animals making their way across the plain.

Before white settlers moved westward, Native Americans hunted bison with bows and arrows for food and for many other uses. They killed only as many animals as they needed.

When the white settlers came, they brought guns. They killed bison for meat and hides, but they often killed many more than they needed. Some settlers killed as many bison as they could. They killed the bison because the animals caused so much trouble for them. The bison ate the grass the settlers needed for their own animals. And bison often ate the crops the settlers were trying to grow. Large herds of bison could knock down fences and even small buildings.

Some of the bison hunters were not settlers. They were meat and hide hunters who killed bison to supply U.S. Army troops and railroad workers. And some bison hunters were sportsmen. These people

The buffalo nickel is the most famous use of the bison as a symbol.

hired guides who knew the West. The guides would take the hunters to the bison herds.

The hunters would kill as many bison as they could with their rifles. On a hunt, one sportsman might kill two thousand bison. A few would be taken back so that their heads could be stuffed and hung on the sportsmen's walls. But most of the dead animals would be left on the plains. Settlers would sometimes collect wagonloads of bison bones to sell. The bones could be used as fertilizer or made into such items as buttons and combs.

As the bison were destroyed, so was the Native Americans' way of life. Without their main source of food, many tribes were forced to move to reservations. There, the U.S. Army provided food for them. But the Native Americans were no longer free.

The bison, often called buffalo, became a symbol of the West. The most famous use of this symbol is on the buffalo nickel. This popular coin is no longer made.

The buffalo nickel was designed by an American sculptor named James Earle Fraser. During the 1870s and 1880s, Fraser lived as a boy in the western Dakota territory, in what is now South Dakota. Fraser later wrote about his life on the prairie and created statues that showed things and people of the West. One of his statues is *The Buffalo Prayer.* He created this statue from a boyhood memory: He had seen a Native American medicine man praying to the Great Spirit for the return of the buffalo.

When Native Americans killed a bison, they used every part of its body in some way.

• Fresh meat was used for food. Meat that could not be eaten was dried, then pounded into powder. Melted fat was added to the powder to make a kind of "bread" called "pemmican." Pemmican could last as long as thirty years.

• Hides were used in many ways. Babies were wrapped in the soft hides of bison calves. Clothing, blankets, and tipi (Indian tent) covers were made from hides. Hides were even used to make buckets and boats.

• Horns were used to make cups and spoons, arrow points, and toys. Ground-up horns were used for medicine.

• Bones made pipes, knives, sled runners, war clubs, paintbrushes, jewelry, toys, and dice.

• Hair was used to make headdresses and ropes. Hair also stuffed pillows and dolls and provided a warm lining for moccasins.

• Even the hooves of the bison were used. In some tribes, they were decorated and hung by the tipi entrance. Visitors to the lodge would rattle the hooves as a kind of doorbell.

The medicine man's prayer was not answered until the twentieth century. Then some laws were passed to protect the American bison, and so their numbers grew. Today bison are raised on some ranches for meat, and there are small wild herds in a few national parks. But huge herds of bison will never again roam free across North America. They will live on only as symbols of a way of life that is gone forever.

CHAPTER

★ 5

A SHINING LIGHT
FOR FREEDOM

The Statue of Liberty stands in New York Harbor. Her real name is Liberty Enlightening the World. She holds a torch high above her head to welcome new Americans to a land where they can be free. She is one of the most important symbols of freedom we have as a nation.

The Statue of Liberty has stood on Liberty Island since 1886. Liberty Island was then called Bedloe's Island. The statue was a gift to the people of America from the people of France. The statue was meant to celebrate the one hundredth birthday of the Declaration of Independence. That birthday came in 1876, almost ten years before the statue was finished.

Opposite:
In 1986, a special country-wide celebration marked the one hundredth birthday of the Statue of Liberty.

33

The French people had helped the American people during the American Revolution. The French wanted to give something to America that would show their continuing friendship. One big problem with giving such a large gift was that it would cost a lot of money. The French government didn't pay for the statue. Instead, the people of France raised the money themselves. Over a ten-year period, they raised $250,000 to pay for the statue.

Making the Statue

The sculptor who was chosen to create the statue was Frédéric Auguste Bartholdi, a Frenchman. Bartholdi sailed to the United States to discuss the statue. His ship arrived in New York Harbor. Bartholdi knew right away that he wanted his statue to stand there, where people coming to America would see it.

The United States also raised money for the project. Americans had to pay for Bedloe's Island and for the base of the statue. Raising the money was not easy. Few Americans were excited about the idea of the statue. But then a newspaper owner named Joseph Pulitzer became interested. He had come to the United States from Hungary in 1864. He remembered what it was like to be a stranger in a new land. He knew the Statue of Liberty would stand in New York Harbor to welcome people to America.

Joseph Pulitzer wanted the statue to be built. He made sure that many articles and cartoons about the

French sculptor
Frédéric Auguste
Bartholdi designed
the Statue of
Liberty.

statue appeared in his newspaper. And he listed the
name of anyone who gave any money for the statue.
He even listed children who gave a few pennies. In
just a few months, Pulitzer's paper, the New York
World, announced that enough money had been
raised. The statue could then be built.

    Bartholdi drew a sketch of a woman with a
crown of rays holding a torch of freedom high above
her head. In her other arm, she held a book with the

The giant Statue of Liberty that stands in New York Harbor is 302 feet tall from its base to its torch.

date July 4, 1776, on it. This was the date of the signing of the Declaration of Independence. The woman wore long, loose robes. She was stepping forward. As she did, she broke chains that had held her feet. These chains had kept her from being free. Her step forward was to show millions of people that they too could be free in America.

It took Bartholdi ten years to create the statue. He needed the help of another artist and engineer, Alexandre Gustave Eiffel. Eiffel, who later designed the famous Eiffel Tower in Paris, France, designed a strong iron skeleton that would hold the metal statue.

Bartholdi first built a nine-foot model of the statue. Next he made a thirty-six-foot model. Finally, he made the full-size statue. It had three hundred sections. The sections were made of copper that was hammered until it was almost as thin as a penny. Once the statue was finished in 1884, it stood in Paris so the French people could see their gift to the United States. Then the statue was taken apart. It was packed into more than two hundred cases for its trip across the Atlantic Ocean.

The statue arrived in the United States on June 17, 1885. Once the base was finished, workers began to build the skeleton of the statue. Then they bolted each copper section of the statue to the skeleton. Finally, at a ceremony in October 1886, U.S. President Grover Cleveland dedicated the statue. He said in his speech, "We will not forget that liberty has made here her home."

THE GIANT STATUE OF LIBERTY

- The Statue of Liberty, from its base to its torch, is 302 feet tall. Visitors who want to climb all the way to the top of the statue must walk up 335 steps. Or they may take an elevator from the ground to the top of the base, then climb 168 steps to the statue's head.
- The statue and the base are equal in height. Each is about 151 feet.
- The base weighs much more than the statue. The base, made of concrete, weighs more than 23,500 tons. The statue itself weighs only about 225 tons.
- Miss Liberty is huge in every way. Her head, from chin to top, is about seventeen feet. Her mouth is three feet wide. And her index finger is eight feet long.

Miss Liberty Lights the Way

The next sixty years were a time when millions of people came to America from Europe. The people who left their homelands to come to the United States were called immigrants. Many immigrants came to America because conditions were so bad in their own countries. Most immigrants to the United States were poor. Often they arrived carrying just a few belongings and speaking no English. In America, they hoped to find freedom and a better life.

About 20 million new Americans arrived as immigrants during the years 1892–1954. Most of these people arrived at an immigration station on Ellis Island. This island is in New York Harbor, right next to the Statue of Liberty. The first glimpse of America that these immigrants had was of Miss Liberty. She held the torch of freedom to light their way.

Alexandre Gustave Eiffel designed the iron skeleton that supports the Statue of Liberty from the inside.

Ellis Island was closed as an immigration station in 1954. Today, a museum there tells the story of the millions of Americans who used Ellis Island as a gateway to America. There is also a museum inside the base of the Statue of Liberty. Visitors may climb steps inside to the top, where they can see for many miles from the windows in the statue's crown.

Visitors also have a chance to read the words of a famous poem on a plaque inside the statue's base. The words are a poem by Emma Lazarus. It is called "The New Colossus." Lazarus wrote the poem to show what the woman with the torch would say if she could speak. In the poem, Miss Liberty says,

> . . . Give me your tired, your poor,
> Your huddled masses yearning to breathe free,
> The wretched refuse of your teeming shore.
> Send these, the homeless, tempest-tosst, to me,
> I lift my lamp beside the golden door.

The poem sends a clear message to people all over the world. It tells them that America will give shelter to anyone who wants freedom. Even the "tired" and "poor" and "homeless" people of other nations will find comfort in America.

The Statue of Liberty still stands as a symbol of the freedom America offers to all people. She lights the way through the golden door of liberty. And she reminds all of us that our country should be a shining light for freedom all over the world.

C H A P T E R

6

OUR
SYMBOLS TODAY

Most of our American symbols have been around for at least two hundred years. Yet they live on today in many ways.

- Many people display flags and bald eagles on their homes. If you look around your house you may find items such as mugs, dish towels, or calendars that have American symbols on them.

- When we go to parades, we stand and cheer as the flag goes by.

- On the Fourth of July, we celebrate our freedom with fireworks and flags. One of the largest Fourth of July celebrations ever held was on the one hundredth birthday of the Statue of Liberty in 1986.

• Each year, many thousands of people make special trips to visit famous symbols such as the Liberty Bell and the Statue of Liberty.

• Advertisers use American symbols to sell products. For example, a fast bike might be advertised with a picture of an American bald eagle. Or a bank might try to attract customers by using the Statue of Liberty in its ads.

In hard times, our symbols become even more important to us. In 1991, for example, the United States was involved in a war against Iraq in the Persian Gulf. People in America wanted to show their support for U.S. troops fighting the war. Many people bought American flags and flew them outside their homes. People bought American flag bumper stickers for their cars and wore flag pins. Many people also displayed another symbol of support for the troops. They tied yellow ribbons around trees, mailboxes, and posts. These yellow ribbons were a reminder of the soldiers who were away. The ribbons would stay up until the troops came home.

During hard times and happy times, our national symbols draw us together as a people. Each of our symbols is special to us as Americans. And each symbol stands for freedom in places all over the world.

When our nation does good deeds, our symbols make us feel proud of our country. If our nation does not do good things, our symbols can make us feel ashamed of our country. Symbols of our nation help us to set goals for what our nation should be.

A sixteen-foot, five-hundred-pound minuteman is pulled down a street in Baltimore, Maryland, before it is displayed in a parade to honor the Constitution.

43

Most of the time, our national symbols make us feel patriotic. They give us a good feeling about living in a land where all the people are free. They give all of us a way to share our pride in our homeland, the United States of America.

Opposite: Patriotic symbols are displayed in Montpelier, Vermont, to show support for troops in the Persian Gulf.

WHY A YELLOW RIBBON?

No one knows for sure where the idea came from of using yellow ribbons as reminders of soldiers who are away. Some people think the idea came from a song that was popular in the 1970s. It was called "Tie a Yellow Ribbon Round the Old Oak Tree." But the first use of yellow ribbons dates back much farther than that.

In the 1600s in England, a song called "All Round My Hat" was popular. This song tells of a woman who wears a willow branch around her hat because her true love is "far, far away." This may be one of the earliest references to tying something around something as a reminder of someone who is away.

During the Civil War, which was fought in the 1860s, soldiers from the South had yellow trim on their uniforms and also wore yellow kerchiefs around their necks. Some stories suggest that soldiers gave these handkerchiefs to their sweethearts before they left to fight.

A song written in 1917 by George Norton was popular during World War I. This song was called "Round Her Neck She Wears a Yellow Ribbon." Later the song was used in a movie titled *She Wore a Yellow Ribbon*, starring John Wayne. The song goes like this:

Around her neck she wore a
   yellow ribbon,
She wore it in the springtime
And the merry month of May
And when they asked her,
Why the yellow ribbon?
She wore it for her lover
   in the U.S. Cavalry,
Far away, far away,
She wore it for her lover
   who was far, far away.

Chronology

1763 British Parliament institutes tax on the American colonies.

1773 Angry colonists in Boston dump tea in the harbor to protest new taxes.

April 19, 1775 Minutemen and British troops exchange the first shots of what would become the Revolutionary War.

July 8, 1776 The Liberty Bell rings out in Philadelphia to celebrate the signing of the Declaration of Independence.

1777 The first flag of the United States is created.

1782 The Great Seal of the United States is adopted, and the bald eagle is named the national bird.

1813 The name "Uncle Sam" is used for the first time in reference to the United States.

1855–1875 The North American bison population is reduced from over 90 million to fewer than one thousand.

October 28, 1886 The Statue of Liberty is dedicated in New York as a symbol of freedom.

For Further Reading

Behrens, June. *Miss Liberty: First Lady of the World.* Chicago: Childrens Press, 1990. *Covers the history of the statue and its significance as a symbol in the United States and to the rest of the world.*

Lepthien, E.U. *Bald Eagles.* Chicago: Childrens Press, 1990. *Discusses the natural habitat and life cycle of America's living symbols.*

Miller, N. *The Liberty Bell.* Chicago: Childrens Press, 1991. *Details the creation and design of this famous symbol of freedom, and explains the many myths surrounding its crack.*

Smith, Carter, ed. *The Revolutionary War.* Brookfield, Connecticut: The Millbrook Press, 1991. *A sourcebook that chronicles the war that inspired so many of America's most enduring symbols.*

Voices From Our Country, A Sourcebook Series. Austin, Texas: Raintree-Steck-Vaughn, 1990. *A collection of poems, essays, songs, and other materials that provide a personal glimpse into America's past.*

Index